Little Wars

Little Wars

Poems by

W. Luther Jett

Cover design by Shay Culligan

ISBN: 978-1-954353-30-5

Kelsay Books
502 South 1040 East, A-119
American Fork, Utah, 84003

I'm gonna lay my sword and shield
down by the riverside

Acknowledgments

Many thanks to the publications in which versions of the following poems have appeared:

Algebra of Owls: "Epitaph"

Beltway Poetry Quarterly—Wartime Issue: "Recessional"

Bourgeon: "A War Story"

JMWW: "Red Dirt"

Spillway: "The Day of Thorns"

The Rockhurst Review: "Physics Lesson"

Third Wednesday: "With an Army at Our Gates"

Tomorrow Magazine: "Black and White (For Bosnia)"

Xanadu: "The Chalk House"

ZZZ Zyne: "And We Fall"

Contents

Recessional

A man is writing a poem
on a very dark night
in a time of war
as planes fly over his head.

He intends it to be a sonnet,
but the meter isn't right,
so he settles for free verse
and keeps writing.

And as he writes, he becomes
conscious of another man
who is also writing a poem
in the middle of a war-torn night.

And with an awareness verging
on vertigo, he realizes
that the poem the other man
is writing is about him.

Indeed, it is about him writing
poetry on a dark night,
and how he—the first man—
is a poem inside another poem.

And the man writing about him
is also a poem, being
written by a third man
on a dark night in wartime.

And it becomes clear—
as clear as things can become
in times of war—that the third
man is also a poem.

The third man is a poem
being written by a fourth man,
and there are poems within poems,
an infinite recessional.

All these poems, being written
by men who are, themselves,
poems within poems
being written by other men.

And this is when the first man
understands that if he is a poem
within a poem within a poem,
then it is all one poem.

One poem with infinite verses
being written with infinite hands
on infinite nights in a time
of infinite war.

And with a clarity that is
only possible when one realizes
that one is a poem inside
a poem the man begins to write:

“A man is writing a poem
“on a very dark night
“in a time of war
“as planes fly over his head . . .”

The Day of Thorns

There was a Day, sharp
and blue—and on either side
of the Day, before and after, Time
was a sheet stretched tight.

And Sarah said, “I pricked my finger
“on that Day. I pricked it
to the bone.” There were Giants, then.
The sky was never again
so blue, so sharp,
nor pulled so tight
you could
snap your finger against it.
Hear it ring.

Storm Bear

The weather had the look
of a bear caught in our headlights
on a back road, looming
where it was never supposed to be,
a hulking cloud, disrupting
all our plans. With great claws,
it scattered sand, wiped away the line
we'd drawn between desire
and circumstance. Roaring,
the storm fell upon us, that bear
running over the mountain to see
what we never wanted to see,
the valley floor trembling,
the echo of distant guns.

Nepenthe

That time we were starving,
one of us died—I
don't remember
whether it was you or
me, but I'm certain
the disappearance tore a hole
in the continuum,
and it doesn't take much
now—fragment
of sky, a wall the colour
of sunflowers, that path
between the birches—miss
one meal and all the other
hungers rush in. Watch
night's fingers grip the naked
trees and see how lights
flicker on only to fade out again.
Yesterday I went
from room to room, all through
the house, rifling drawers,
unsealing boxes, searching
for what cannot be found.
For what
I have forgotten.

Poppies

Flesh cuts steel,
steel bleeds carnivalglass—
        rubies
litter the moist, dark earth.

The Front burns here,
along the narrow ridge—
        but not there
where slumbering wheat
        rolls westward.

If you crouch low,
very low, your ear
        pressed
to the cold stones——

You will hear them
from a distance
        —the big guns—
how they tremble the air
        of the morning.

Flesh cuts steel, steel
bleeds carnivalglass—
        red tears
water the waking soil.

Vanishing Point / *Ach Du*

Oh you, and you, and you
with your little wars—
What do I know?

I was on my way to the dry-cleaners
when the news came—No,
I was making coffee and—No,
no, I had just stepped out the door

when the phone rang, the radio
announcer interrupted my favorite
song, the planes flew over too low,
they rattled my windows.

And you, and you, and no,
I didn't know—
the war inside you, the war

You didn't know, you had just
stepped outside to take a call—
Yes, and the planes—Yes,
then the coffee went cold,

milk turned sour, that song
you were writing—the window
shattered, spray of glass, and you,
and you, and I, and no—

We didn't know there are no
little wars—no distance
we cannot reduce to nothing.

A War Story

Here is the book
with torn pages.
Only half remains
to be deciphered.

And here is the house
with burnt rooms,
and a few fading photos
scattered across the floor.

And here, here—Forgive me
but these are my bones.
This is the face I was using.
Wrap them all tenderly.

Sing of me as you sleep.

Epitaph

You wrote my name in stone,
graved it in brass, called me
hero because
that day fire
dropt from the sky
to brand our city, I was
there and did
only what wanted doing.

No more.

And all your flags and flowers—
I never lived to see. Your songs,
those speeches,
the medals—
that morning I wasn't looking
for any of that.
That day
I only wanted
to get through it.
I didn't.
And I would give anything

not
to be
your hero.

Physics Lesson

There is some fragment
of Eternity lodged
between two wooden
fence-slats on Constitution
Avenue where last night—
under stars that know
nothing of Chemistry,
Physics, or the ways
carbon atoms conspire
to make war on
one another or to make
love—we kissed
as if by melding our
mouths together
we might hold back the
sun—might hold
back the bombers, hold
back the guns.

Rio America, Autumn, 1994

There is a lake
and there is a highway
and the sky is reflected in the lake
and the wind moves over the blue waters.

There is a tall building
beside the lake and a path that circles
the lake and the cars pass on the highway
and people are walking on the path around the lake
and it is autumn, and the sun shines on the lake
and on the building, on the people and on the cars
passing on the highway in the afternoon.

And we do not know
who lives in the building
and we do not know
how the lake came to be here
between the building and the highway
and we do not know
how long the sun will shine
and we do not know
where all the cars are going, we
do not know where we are going
or how long it will take
and we do not know who
we are, only that
we are, and the lake is,
and the highway is,
and the building and the path
and the wind and the sun, this
autumn day in America.

With an Army at Our Gates

Even up to the final moment
before the walls of the city
collapse, people
go about their usual
business: A man
washes out his socks in the sink;
someone runs to catch the subway;
a girl in a café orders salad
while thinking about the argument
she just had with her lover;
two professional rivals
meet on the street and
nod politely; it looks like rain;
a mother opens the back door
to call her children in for lunch;
an old man coughs
waiting in line for a matinée;
the phone rings—
it is a wrong number.
All, as if the day
were no different
from any other: As if
an army of men without faces
were not at our gates.
A lone honeybee pollinates
a red, red flower;
a little girl starts singing
and refuses to stop; she sings
even up to the final moment.
Even after it.

The Chalk House

After the guns
stopped and I began
to see that I was saved,
and thought I might
crawl out of the latrine that was
my cradle—When the air
fell silent, the small rains driving
down the dust to ground,
they collected us
from the cellars and broomclosets,
from alleycorners
and from blasted fields,
brought us to this place of rooms
and open windows empty
as a belly. Where I could not
sleep from weariness,
with the way the long night went
unpunctuated—waiting
for the siren's blast, the tramp
of boots along the stair,
that never came. And morning
brought the song of spoons,
and soft-voiced men who said:

Child, Child,
Draw us your house, the house
Where you were born.

And I could not.
The edges would not form,
nor walls nor windows—None
could I recall. I stood
cold chalk in hand before the slate,
scrawling misshapen circles
on the black ground.

A house
no architect could dare
design—All broken curves
and scattered line—a dizzy,
tangled mass of strokes,
all adding up to Nothing
but a sprawl of holes,
and not one deep enough
to crawl inside.

Note: "The Chalk House" is an ekphrastic, based upon a poignant photograph taken by David "Chim" Seymour in 1948. The photograph depicts a child refugee called "Tereska", after she was asked to draw her house. The photograph may be seen on display at the Boston Museum of Fine Arts.

Mostar

When a bridge too narrow for
dreams falls into a river
too deep for tears,
what is left behind?

On your side, you hold a
bucket; on my side,
I guard the well;
above us—broken horns
of an autumn moon.

V-E Day

When we won the war, the dead
stirred in their silent,
hidden graves. If there could be
breath to utter speech,
if we could support
the absurdity of corpses
rising to speak, with what words
might they judge those nights
of fire, empty days, the dust
of summer formed from mud of spring,
the cities leveled and the fields
upchurned—bodies vaporized, bones
covering the grass? None,
save the wind harping vacant
rib-cages, a great sigh
to harrow a blasted continent.

Black and White

For Bosnia

This little village
sleeps; a black and white
landscape, where snow
has erased autumn's
weeds. The stars
cannot be seen tonight. Once
in another sleeping
village, red came to
shatter black and white
dreams, drenching them, then
freezing them forever in
ice and fog. Dreams
are not lies, only
shadows of a hidden
star. Snow, weeds, sleep:
These, too, are not lies, not
meant to be dismissed
with a gesture, with the wave
of a riding crop—left,
right, left—but the world
is not made of only black
and white. Red comes—
no lie. Fog, ice—these
are not lies either.
I can't tell you what
is a lie, and what
is truth, unless you can
understand why neither
black nor white nor red are
lies. Unless you understand
that all villages
are one village, all
dreams, one dream, all men,

all women—dreamers. I
should show you lies,
to help you recognize what
truth is? Not when
all that's needed
is to recognize a liar. Black
and white, sometimes,
are what the world screams
when its night is split
in two by red.

Red Dirt

This is the hell of it, the injury
becomes apparent in each step
across the beaten earth,
the wound we make of breathing.
There is no life which, in the end
does not depend on death.

Carnivore cells
consume all in their paths; fungus
feeds upon decay; even flowers
cannot bloom by sunlight's
sole behest, requiring rot,
broken leaves and faded petals.

Do you imagine to do better
than the poppies of the field?
You who scatter seed
across continents? Each orgasm
is a little death. Each song
a requiem. Simply rising
of a morning is to undertake
a battle, pitched against unending night.
Red dirt collects
in every crevice of the skin
and never will scrub clean.

The soldier in his bivouac
dreams himself at war with time
and starts awake to scan
a ragged horizon, marking the slow
paling down the sky—neither
he nor I nor you can claim
to know the day ahead, although

the watcher on the border
watching back we know
well as we know our selves.

And We Fall

. . . over and over, until
the trees no longer shake
their leaves in prayer, and the earth
can no longer bear
to receive us—until the wind
no longer sobs, and the iron sky has
no more tears—
until the sea and the land forget
that they are rivals—until the stones
refuse to mark
our passage anymore, and we are
forced to admit, we have no one to
blame for this—
that the smoke blinding us, the ash
clinging to our teeth, and the steel tears
searing flesh—all
are ours, ours, and ours alone, our making
because we refuse to make stars
out of the coals
that burn in our hearts—because, instead,
we choose to make wars . . .

About the Author

W. Luther Jett is a native of Montgomery County, Maryland and a retired special educator. His poetry has been published in numerous journals, such as *The GW Review, Beltway, Innisfree, Potomac Review,* and *Little Patuxent Review,* as well as several anthologies, including *My Cruel Invention* and *Written in Arlington.* His poetry performance piece, "Flying to America," debuted at the 2009 Capital Fringe Festival in Washington D.C. Luther is also the facilitator of a monthly virtual open mike sponsored by the Hyattstown Mill Arts Project in Hyattstown, Maryland, as well as a poetry workshop that meets the first Saturday of every month.

In addition to the work you hold in your hands, Luther is the author of three poetry chapbooks: *Not Quite: Poems Written in Search of My Father* (Finishing Line Press, 2015) and *Our Situation* (Prolific Press, 2018), and *Everyone Disappears* (Finishing Line Press, 2020).

www.ingramcontent.com/pod-product-compliance
Lightning Source LLC
LaVergne TN
LVHW020050110826
845155LV00029B/713